Real Bible Believers

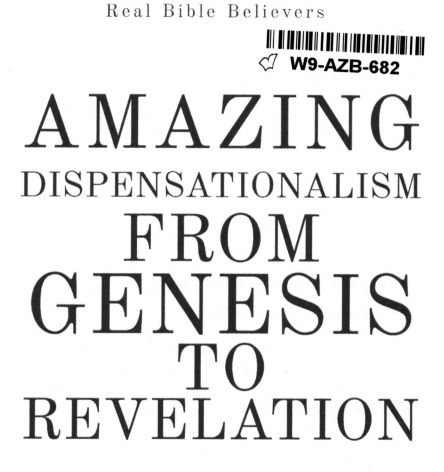

W9-AZB-682

AMAZING
DISPENSATIONALISM
FROM
GENESIS
TO
REVELATION

G.H. KIM

Names: Gene, Kim, author.

Title: Amazing Dispensationalism From Genesis to Revelation. A Christian's guide to rightly divide the word of God.

Description: Why is it so hard to understand and read the Bible?

We often think that we need to understand Greek and Hebrew in order to understand the essence of the Bible. But this is not true! Kim shows us how we can read the Bible and interpret it without a degree in theology, the secret is to believe what the Bible says.

Study to shew thyself approved unto God, a workman that needeth not to be ashamed, rightly dividing the word of truth. 2 Timothy 2:15

God is the same, from everlasting to everlasting. But, the way God deals with us changes. Kim walks us through the different people in different timelines from the book of Genesis all the way to the book of Revelation. God is an orderly God and there is no contradiction within the word of God.

How do we reconcile the verses in New Testament that tell us that we need works to show our faith, and another that tells us that nothing that can take our salvation away?

What does the book of Revelation mean?

Is the whole Bible metaphorical and not to be taken seriously?

This book is a Bible-based read to help anyone understand how to read the Bible. You will be surprised afterwards how easy it is to understand God's word and discover His perfect will for you.

Subjects: Religion & Spirituality | Christian Books & Bibles | Reference & Interpretation | Bible Study & Reference | Handbooks | Bible Study

www.realbiblebelievers.com

ANONYMOUS COMMENTS TAKEN FROM OUR YOUTUBE CHANNEL ABOUT THIS TEACHING

ↄ⌒ↄ⌒

"I feel so free, finally I understand dispensationalism, I had no idea! Thank you so much - God bless you!!! I have learned more in the last hour and 1/2 than I have in 50 years! :)"

"This is definitely lacking in the churches today. Dispensationalism is under strong attack and yet it is so clearly seen in God's Word."

"This is so far the best preaching I have ever had. It totally clears up my questions about Salvation. One thing I don't understand is why my pastor doesn't teach such truth. I have to say most of Christians in my Church don't know this beautiful truth."

"Dispensational teaching was probably the best teaching I have encountered in studying the Bible and has helped me greatly to understand and will also blow the atheists away

when they come with their 1001 apparent contradictions in the Scriptures. Thank you and God bless you."

"Lordship salvation was killing my joy. I'm so glad you have opened my eyes through God's Spirit to these doctrines that I had no idea were so wrong. Now the warfare has changed dramatically in my inner being and for the better!!"

"Thirty years a Christian, and did not understand how to rightly divide. TYSM!!!"

"Wow, this makes me want to study my Bible now!"

"People who just read Bible for curiosity's sake, usually conclude that Bible is contradicting itself, because they don't understand dispensationalism. Everyone should start Bible study from your sermon, Pastor! Excellent teaching!"

CONTENTS

INTRODUCTION

―――――――― ༉ ༉ ――――――――

This book will be about dispensationalism. Many wrong doctrines are present today. When seeking correct doctrine, dispensationalism will be a core starting principle. To find truth in the scriptures, you must rightly divide it.

> *"Study to shew thyself approved unto God, a workman that needeth not to be ashamed, rightly dividing the word of truth." (2 Timothy 2:15)*

Dispensationalism is a system of dividing the Word.

According to Webster's 1828 dictionary, **dispensationalism** refers to the administration of different matters to different groups of people.

Studying the different groups to which God gave His different doctrines will remedy a variety of issues and aid in discerning which do or do not apply personally to you.

CREATION
- ADAM

Genesis 1–3

───────── ༄ ─────────

T he ages begin with Adam (Genesis 1–3). In this age, salvation is by works, as seen when God said to Adam and Eve that if they eat the fruit of knowledge of good and evil they "shalt surely die" (Genesis 2:16–17). Hence, salvation by grace through faith alone was not active at this time and did not hold throughout all ages.

CONSCIENCE
- NOAH AND ABRAHAM

Genesis 4–50, Job

———————— ༄༅ ————————

In this age, salvation is by faith and works under conscience, for "the doers of the law shall be justified" (Romans 2:13). Our conscience knows what is right and wrong, and to follow our conscience is to follow the law (Romans 2:14–15).

Noah was one person who was saved in this manner. In his time, all of mankind and their consciences were corrupted (Genesis 6:5) with the only exception being Noah, who was "a just man," "walked with God," and "found grace in the eyes of the Lord" (Genesis 6:8–9).

Noah's salvation was based on his construction of the ark. If he did not live rightly with God or build the ark, he would have been no different from the other lost people. Hence, his salvation is different from Christians today since none of us built an ark and many of us frequently grieve our consciences.

Abraham was another person who had faith and works under a right conscience. To say that his salvation was like us Christians is also wrong, for Abraham was "justified by works when he had offered Isaac his son..." (James 2:21–23), and his

5

faith had to be perfected by his works. His salvation was not by faith alone (James 2:24).

PHYSICAL ISRAEL AND COVENANT THEOLOGY

<hr>

∂᠎᠎᠎᠎᠎

Abraham is the father of physical Israel, and God made an everlasting covenant with the physical nation of Israel (Genesis 17:7–8), just as the people who God led out of Egypt were the physical Jews (Judges 2:1).

There is a heresy called replacement theology, which believes that the Christian church has replaced the nation of Israel, but this isn't true because the covenant with Abraham is everlasting, and God will "never break (His) covenant with (the Jews)" (Judges 2:1).

Covenant theology, on the other hand, believes that salvation by grace is and will be the same ever since Adam's fall to the end. This is nonsense as Abraham and Noah's salvation was dependent on works. Calvinists generally believe in this.

Some KJV-only independent fundamental Baptists subscribe to this as well while still calling themselves dispensational. Real dispensationalists do not follow this heresy because covenant theology is the enemy camp of dispensationalism.

SPIRITUAL AND PHYSICAL DEALINGS

I n the Old Testament, God dealt with His people both physically and spiritually. But what is vital to understand is that throughout the Old Testament, it was primarily physical dealings. When Adam died, his spirit died. Hence, God could not deal with man spiritually.

From this, it also makes sense why Noah and Abraham had to do physical works to gain salvation. They could not be saved by faith alone in Jesus Christ because that is spiritual. We Christians who possess a lively spiritual nature can do so.

The foundation of God's dealings is physical. But this does not mean there were no spiritual dealings in the Old Testament. Throughout Genesis 4–50 and the entire book of Job, God did deal with people not only physically but also spiritually. Abraham, for example, received the imputed righteousness of God not by works but when his belief in the Lord was "counted (to) him for righteousness" (Genesis 15:5–6).

The Apostle Paul also referred to some Old Testament verses to prove spiritual Christian doctrines. Paul mentions that "Abraham believed God and it was counted unto him for righteousness" (Romans 4:2–3). Notice how Paul was able to argue to the Jews that Abraham was counted righteous by faith, not by works.

CONFUSION REGARDING ABRAHAM AND WORKS

༂ﻬ༂ﻬ

S ome Hyper-dispensationalists believe there was no salvation by grace that excluded works in the Old Testament. This is especially seen in James where it is written that Abraham was 'justified by works' (James 2:21-24). What is lacking in this argument is proper division. Genesis 15 clearly shows Abraham received salvation by faith, and there were no works involved. Abraham's salvation by works took place many years afterward when he was ready to sacrifice Isaac (James 2).Hence, by dividing the times, there is no contradiction.

Hyper-dispensationalists tend to diminish God's spiritual dealings before the Church Age.This is heresy, as Paul himself raised spiritual dealings found in the Old Testament (Romans 4:2–3). If the hyper-dispensationalists are correct, Paul would be a liar. We must, therefore, be acquainted with the spiritual dealings in the Old Testament.

THE LAW
- MOSES AND DAVID

Exodus to Malachi

———————— ꙮ ————————

Jews during Moses' time had to follow the law of Moses. It was also their plan of salvation. It is written in Deuteronomy that if Israel forgot God, they were counted as "children in whom is no faith" (Deuteronomy 32:18–20). God did not count them as people of faith if they failed to remember God. Compare this to the Christian church today—how many have forgotten God in their walk?

If the Jews under Mosaic law have "forgotten God that formed (them)" and "provoke (Him) to anger with their vanities," God will also send unto them a fire that "(burns) unto the lowest hell" (Deuteronomy 32:18, 21–22). In other words, if they fail in their works and forget God, they will burn in hell.

Compare this to Psalms 9 where it is written, "The wicked shall be turned into hell, and all the nations that forget God" (Psalms 9:17). Hence, for Moses and the Jews, salvation was by faith and works.

David also realized that he could lose the Holy Spirit for his salvation by his sin (Psalms 51:11–12). See that David was concerned with losing his salvation. It is different for us

Christians who believe that we cannot lose the Holy Spirit even if we fail in our works.

PROSPERITY GOSPEL?

$\partial\Omega\sigma$

Notice that physical prosperity for the Jews was invoked by their physical works (1 Kings 2:3). There is a heresy regarding this called the prosperity gospel that you should avoid. Modern preachers such as Joel Osteen say that if you give money to God and do physical good works, God will richly bless your life.

Even in the majority of Christians, this holds untrue. Many Christians serve God rightly and find greater hardship and suffering instead of success. But the main problem with this teaching is that they are taking a doctrine meant for a different time period and group of people—Old Testament Jews—and applying it wrongly.

SIGNS AND WONDERS FOR THE JEW

---∂૭∂૭---

Since God physically dealt with physical Jews, He had to prove His power by way of physical signs and wonders. God gave the Jews signs through Moses with the intent being that they may believe him (Exodus 4:1–9).

CHRISTIANS AND THE MOSAIC LAW

───────── ༄ ༄ ༄ ─────────

W hat is important to note is that even when Old Testament Jews follow the law, their works are considered imperfect to God. Paul writes that "by the deeds of the law there shall no flesh be justified in (God's) sight" (Romans 3:20).

For Christians today, we have Jesus' sacrifice on the cross, which is perfect unlike the works of the law where "now the righteousness of God without the law is manifested...by faith of Jesus Christ" (Romans 3:21–22).

On a side note, this argument is powerful in convincing Jews who subscribe to Old Testament doctrines today that they cannot be saved by their law but only through Jesus. In fact, Jews today do not keep the law in their lowering of standards of blood sacrifice and circumcision, which were both necessary in the law. This also debunks the hyper-dispensational argument that there is nothing applicable for the Christian in the Old Testament because Christians can use this comparison with the Old Testament to show Jews their failure of works and need of a perfect salvation by faith in the Lord.

Apart from the Mosaic Law comparison, a Christian can also use the example of David as an exception to salvation by works. He broke the law of Moses in committing adultery and murder. He deserved death yet was spared by God. Paul writes that David was a man "unto whom God imputeth righteousness without works" (Romans 4:6). This did not mean, however, that he disregarded the truth during his time of both faith and works being required for salvation, as seen throughout Psalms about David's relationship with God.

THE FIRST COMING - JOHN THE BAPTIST AND JESUS

Matthew to John

―――――⟨δ ᖶ δᖶ⟩―――――

THE MESSIAH AS KING AND SUFFERER

The Messiah is prophesied to come as King and Sufferer (Isaiah 52:13–15). God's servant will be as a king as "he shall be exalted and extolled, and be very high," (Isaiah 52:13) while also being as a sufferer where "his visage was so marred more than any man, and his form more than the sons of men" (Isaiah 52:14). Furthermore, he shall "sprinkle many nations" (Isaiah 52:15), and "the kings shall shut their mouths at him" (Isaiah 52:16), implying the servant will be as a messianic king. Not considering Jesus as King and Sufferer will lead to a vast number of wrong doctrines.

Note that Old Testament Jews believe that the coming of the Messiah will be as one coming only, not as a first and second coming. Without dispensationalism and the belief in dividing the Word, you will be no different in your belief from an Old Testament Jew. Their belief is only part of an incomplete bigger picture.

WATER BAPTISM AND WORKS REPENTANCE

When John the Baptist arrived, water baptism and works repentance were both involved for salvation (Matthew 3:1–12). You will go to hell if you do not bring forth "fruits meet for repentance" (Matthew 3:8), and baptism had to be performed (Matthew 3:6).

Paul Washer, Ray Comfort, and Lordship Salvationists believe you have to repent for salvation. We also believe this, but the difference is they believe that works are involved—that after being saved by faith, your life should be cleansed of sin and filled with good works. This belief is based on Matthew 3:1–12, but they fail to see this was Jews in that particular time period while Christians are many years into the future in the Church Age.

THE KINGDOM OF HEAVEN

The kingdom of heaven is a physical kingdom. During His first coming, Jesus mentioned this kingdom quite often.

Note, however, that because God was handling the Jews physically, it cannot refer to "going to heaven" but must be a physical earthly kingdom. Remember the plenteous prophecies of the Messiah as King—the Jews expected an earthly king with an earthly ruler.

In Matthew, it is written that "the kingdom of heaven suffereth violence, and the violent take it by force" (Matthew 11:12). Violent people on earth cannot take away heaven. Hence, the verse has to refer to the fight for a physical earthly kingdom.

Jesus himself preached the kingdom of heaven to the physical Jews, for he "went about all Galilee, teaching in their synagogues, and preaching the gospel of the kingdom" (Matthew 4:23). Jesus did not preach the gospel of Christ or any other gospel because the Jews were looking for the Messiah as a king.

During the Sermon on the Mount, Jesus preached the physical kingdom where he said, "Blessed are the poor in spirit; for theirs is the kingdom of heaven" (Matthew 5:3). He also outlines their plan of salvation to enter the earthly kingdom where he mentions that "except (their) righteousness shall exceed the righteousness of the scribes and Pharisees, (they) shall in no case enter into the kingdom of heaven" (Matthew 5:20). In other words, a person's work in being an upright person has to exceed the works of the religious leaders. This is a massive amount of work. The reason for the large emphasis on work is because God was physically dealing with the physical Jews, and physical works of righteousness have to be involved in their salvation. Hence, works are involved for salvation in this physical kingdom.

Jesus also proclaims this in Matthew 5:22:

> *"Whosoever is angry with his brother without a cause shall be in danger of the judgment: and whosoever shall say to his brother, Raca, shall be in danger of the council: but whosoever shall say, Thou fool, shall be in danger of hell fire."*

This is not Christian doctrine because it bears the context of the physical kingdom. If God was ruling over physical people on earth, all of His subjects would be saints, and it would be wrong for His people to call each other fools.

Today, however, there are plenty of fools. Paul called false prophets "fools," and Jesus called the Pharisees "fools." This verse only makes sense if we will go to hell for saying "fool," and this is true if God was ruling earth right now with His saints.

ON END TIMES

———— ⸎ ————

J esus talked about end-time Jewish matters in Matthew 24. This is important because he mentioned works for salvation and a post-tribulation rapture. This will not be for spiritual Christians. It is Jewish.

The disciples asked Jesus about what would happen in the end-times (Matthew 24:3). Jesus did mention that "he that shall endure unto the end, the same shall be saved" (Matthew 24:13), meaning physical works are involved for salvation during the end-times.

Following the context of verse 16—"Then let them which be in Judaea flee into the mountains" —we know the following verses are for the Jews.

Jesus says, "woe unto them that are with child, and to them that give suck in those days" (Matthew 24:19). Those with children in the tribulation will have a woeful time. After the tribulation, there will be a rapture, as after the tribulation the angels sent by the Son of Man "shall gather together His elect from the four winds, from one end of heaven to the other" (Matthew 24:29–31). This rapture will be for the Jews, not the spiritual Christian.

A heresy exists in the Christian church called the post-tribulation rapture. They believe Christians will go through the tribulation and will be raptured afterward. They think the church will be raptured before the wrath of God but still go through the tribulation. It is heretical because the tribulation is for the Jews.

Furthermore, Scripture shows that the wrath of God refers to the tribulation. Luke 21, parallel to Matthew 24, writes for those in Judaea to "flee to the mountains" (Luke 21:21). Hence, the verses following Luke 21:21 also refer to the tribulation. Luke 21:23 refers to the time period of tribulation as "wrath," which suggests that the tribulation is also called God's wrath. Therefore, what post-tribbers argue—that Christians will go through the tribulation yet be raptured before God's wrath—does not make sense because God's wrath refers to the tribulation.

TRANSITION FROM PHYSICAL TO SPIRITUAL DEALINGS

---- ༄༅ ----

J esus Christ was born of the Holy Ghost. Thus, he has the authority to introduce spiritual teachings. There is also a gradual transition throughout the ages from physical to spiritual dealings. During Jesus's first coming, He was still introducing spiritual things, but the majority of His dealings were still Jewish and physical.

Bible Believers teach there was a transition from physical to spiritual, from Jesus and His apostles to Paul. The dealings after the transition are spiritual.

Why was there a transition?

It came about because physical Israel was going to reject Jesus, which made God turn to the Church. However, this was not an immediate change from the Jews to the Church. It was a gradual transition, because God did not immediately cut off Israel. He was being merciful by gradually cutting them off with many chances to repent. The gradual transition was finally finished when we reach after the timeline of Paul.

Jesus has the authority to introduce spiritual doctrines. In John, it is written, "But the hour cometh, and now is, when the true worshippers shall worship the Father in spirit and in truth: for the Father seeketh such to worship him" (John 4:23). Jesus clearly says the hour will come when our dealings with God will be spiritual. Hence, spiritual dealings are forming during Jesus's time period, and from Matthew to John, you would find both spiritual Christian doctrines and Jewish doctrines, the latter being as God was still dealing with the Jews.

Another instance where Jesus did something spiritual was in Luke when he said to a woman, "Thy faith hath saved thee" and forgives her of her sins because of her faith (Luke 7:47–50). That is a spiritual Christian doctrine that sins are forgiven by faith and not by works.

You will also find Jesus talking about a spiritual kingdom called the kingdom of God. Remember that the kingdom of heaven is physical and different from the spiritual kingdom of God. Jesus says that "the kingdom of God is within you" (Luke 17:21), proving that the kingdom is spiritual because a physical kingdom cannot go inside you.

Notice that Jesus first dealt with Jews, then transitions to Gentiles afterwards. Jesus commands his disciples to "Go not into the way of the Gentiles, and into any city of the Samaritans enter ye not: But go rather to the lost sheep of the house of Israel" (Matthew 10:5–6). This clearly shows that Jesus' ministry—and by extension the apostles' ministry—was primarily Jewish. Hence, there will be plenty of physical dealings while spiritual dealings will be rarer.

Jesus also warned the Jews that the kingdom of God would be taken from them and given to a Gentile nation if the Jews rejected Jesus. This is seen in Matthew when Jesus said, "The kingdom of God shall be taken from you, and given to a nation bringing forth the fruits thereof" (Matthew 21:43). Hence, God's focus was gradually brought away from the Jew and given to the Gentile.

THE CHURCH AGE

PART 1
- APOSTLES

Acts and James to Revelation

———— ꙮ ————

Right now, we are under the Church Age. At the beginning of the Church Age, spiritual and physical dealings were intermingled as God transitioned between the physical Jews and the spiritual Church.

It is important to understand that the apostles' ministry was primarily Jewish. In Galatians, it is written, "For he that wrought effectually in Peter to the apostleship of the circumcision..." (Galatians 2:8), showing that Peter's apostleship was to the Jews, who are the circumcision. Paul writes, "that we should go unto the heathen, and they unto the circumcision" (Galatians 2:9), with "they" referring to James, Cephas, and John, who are apostles. Thus, the apostles' ministry will be primarily Jewish with some spiritual doctrines.

This is different from Christians. The reason why the apostles talk so frequently about end-time events is because the apostles were taught under Jesus' ministry that often mentioned the end times.

WORKS FOR SALVATION IN THE GENERAL EPISTLES

$\backsim \curvearrowright \backsim$

Regarding James the apostle, his writings contain little Christian doctrine. In James 1:1, he dedicates his writings "to the twelve tribes which are scattered abroad." Hence, the book of James will contain Jewish doctrines and teachings.

The end-times are mentioned in James 5:3: "Your gold and silver is cankered, and the rust of them shall be a witness against you, and shall eat your flesh as it were fire. Ye have heaped treasure together for the last days." With the context of the Jew and the end-times, the Jew's plan of salvation will be, like Jesus said during His ministry, faith and works. With this in mind, it makes sense that James writes, "Ye see then how that by works a man is justified, and not by faith only" (James 2:24).

Peter writes, "Forasmuch as ye know that ye were not redeemed with corruptible things, as silver and gold, from your vain conversation received by tradition from your fathers..." (1 Peter 1:18). Since it mentions a tradition learned by their forefathers, it is likely Jewish. The end-times are mentioned as he writes Christ "was manifest in these last times for you" (1 Peter 1:20). If it is end-times and Jewish, salvation will be by works: "And if the righteous scarcely be saved, where shall the ungodly and the sinner appear?" (1

Peter 4:18). This implies you would barely be saved by being a righteous person while the wicked are lost. This is works for salvation.

John writes about the end-times as well: "Little children, it is the last time; and as ye have heard that antichrist shall come, even now are there many antichrists; whereby we know that it is the last time" (1 John 2:18). We know John ministered to Jews primarily, and if it is the end-times, the salvation plan will be works.

"We know that we have passed from death unto life, because we love the brethren. He that loveth not his brother abideth in death" (1 John 3:14). Do saved Christians have to start loving each other to retain their salvation? Definitely not. Many Christians do not love their brother and yet are still saved by faith alone.

PHYSICAL SIGNS FOR SALVATION?

---∂୧∂୧---

I f the apostles' ministries were primarily Jewish, it would be primarily physical as well. It is coherent that they would speak frequently about water baptism, healing signs, and physical actions to receive the baptism of the Holy Ghost. Signs and speaking in tongues come from the book of Acts: "And they were all filled with the Holy Ghost, and began to speak with other tongues, as the Spirit gave them utterance" (Acts 2:4).

There exists a heresy known as the signs movement, subscribed to by Charismatics and Pentecostals. They believe you have to speak in tongues and receive the baptism of the Holy Ghost from the laying of hands. This is heresy because we are in a time period that is later than Acts 2.

Acts 2 also referred to Jews in particular as "Jerusalem Jews" (Acts 2:5). The reason why Acts 2 only applied to Jews was because they are a physical people, and God deals physically with the Jews. Water baptism, signs, and receiving the baptism of the Holy Spirit are physical actions, not spiritual. Hence, they are for the Jews only.

Many have quoted Acts 2:38 for their salvation, "Then Peter said unto them, Repent, and be baptized every one of you in the name of Jesus Christ for the remission of sins, and ye shall receive the gift of the Holy Ghost." Pentecostals and those in the Church of Christ believe this verse, that water baptism is required for salvation and the Holy Spirit baptism. Again, this is for Jews and not the Christians because Jews are dealt with physically.

SPIRITUAL DEALINGS FROM THE APOSTLES

———— ⟋⟍⟍⟍ ————

Even though the apostles' dealings were primarily Jewish, they taught some spiritual Christian administrations as well. Acts 15:9 says, "And put no difference between us and them, purifying their hearts by faith." This implies both Gentiles and Jews are saved by faith with no difference.

It is followed by Acts 15:10: "Now therefore why tempt ye God, to put a yoke upon the neck of the disciples, which neither our fathers nor we were able to bear?" This implies works will not save. Afterward, that salvation is by faith and not works, which is made clear in Acts 15:11, "But we believe that through the grace of the Lord Jesus Christ we shall be saved, even as they."

The Apostles all agree that salvation is by faith without works. Regarding the command of "ye must be circumcised, and keep the law," they "gave no such commandment" (Acts 15:23–24). What the apostles have said thus annulled those who teach among Christians that salvation involves works. Do not fear when someone tries to prove salvation is by works—salvation involves both faith and works only for Jews in the end-times.

In Acts 8, an apostle taught Christian doctrine. The eunuch that Philip baptized was saved like us Christians because he believed on Jesus Christ for his salvation first before his baptism (Acts 8:36–38).

The Apostle John also mentions doctrine that would apply to the spiritual Christian church where it is written to Gaius, "Which have borne witness of thy charity before the church..." (3 John 6). The church is mentioned. Hence, 3 John will contain some Christian doctrine.

And 1 Peter is especially rich in Christian doctrine. It is written, "To an inheritance incorruptible, and undefiled, and that fadeth not away, reserved in heaven for you, Who are kept by the power of God through faith unto salvation ready to be revealed in the last time" (1 Peter 1:4–5). As it mentions, there is something in heaven that is reserved that will never fade away. It implies you cannot lose heaven due to faith. This is a spiritual Christian doctrine.

PART 2
- PAUL

Acts, Hebrews, and Romans to Philemon

———————— ∂૭∂૭ ————————

THE APOSTLE PAUL

Many are confused as to the mingling of physical, Jewish end-time and spiritual Christian doctrine. There is a mingling because the apostles were trained by Jesus to perform a primarily Jewish ministry, and Jesus's ministry comprises doctrines for both the end-time Jew and the spiritual Christian. Thus, we have to examine each verse to see who it applies to, and it will never be the case that a book is only for the Jew or Christian. This sounds daunting, but we can know it through the Apostle Paul. He wrote the majority of the passages that apply to the spiritual Christian church.

For any writings from Jesus or the apostles, if they contradict Paul, it applies to a different group of people at a different time. This is the way to read the Bible. Matthew to John applies to, primarily, Jews. This is also the case for books like Acts and the General Epistles from James to Revelation. If

41

something within these books contradicts Paul, it would be end-time Jewish doctrine.

Why is it that Paul's doctrine is distinctly for the spiritual Christian church? His ministry is primarily for the Gentile and is not tied to the physical dealings of the Jews. Paul writes, "For I speak to you Gentiles, inasmuch as I am the apostle of the Gentiles, I magnify mine office" (Romans 11:13). This clearly shows his ministry is for the Gentiles, which explains why his writings are so different. He is not sitting under Jesus's ministry in preaching about the end-times to the Jews.

Paul also said that his gospel was a revelation from God and was unknown to all other time periods: "Now to him that is of power to stablish you according to my gospel, and the preaching of Jesus Christ, according to the revelation of the mystery, which was kept secret since the world began" (Romans 16:25) Hence, Paul's gospel is new.

PAUL'S GOSPEL

———————— ༄ ༅ ————————

Remember that Jewish teachings say that faith and works are both required for salvation. Paul says that salvation is by faith without works and a person is still saved no matter what sin is committed. Unlike Old Testament Jews who are afraid of losing salvation when they do evil works, Paul says you are saved by faith regardless of whether you perceive yourself to be saved after evil works.

"And if by grace, then is it no more of works: otherwise grace is no more grace. But if be of works, then it is no more grace: otherwise work is no more work" (Romans 11:6) This verse says if you are saved by grace, it would be by grace alone, and if it were works, it would be by works alone. If not, the meanings of works and faith would have been voided.

Paul Washer, Ray Comfort, and many others teach a ridiculous idea that salvation is by faith, but a person is not truly saved if sinning remains constant. That is not Paul's salvation by grace—works is not faith. Works and faith must be separate.

In Ephesians, it states, "And grieve not the holy spirit of God, whereby ye are sealed unto the day of redemption" (Ephesians 4:30). This explains that you can sin against the Holy Spirit and grieve God yet remain saved, or "sealed unto the day of redemption".

43

Remember that Paul was given a revelation that had never been taught before. One of these revelations is that there would be a rapture apart from the tribulation wrath. Jesus taught a rapture that occurs after the tribulation—Paul taught of a rapture that will not be within the tribulation but before it. "For God hath not appointed us to wrath..." (1 Thess. 5:9). As God will not put us in a time of wrath—referring to the tribulation—Christians will not go through the tribulation.

Paul again talks about a pre-tribulation rapture in 1 Corinthians 15:51–52:

> *"And behold I shew you a mystery; We shall not all sleep, but we shall all be changed, In a moment, in the twinkling of an eye, at the last trump: for the trumpet shall sound, and the dead shall be raised incorruptible, and we shall be changed."*

Paul mentions in this passage about a rapture that nobody knew before. Since this rapture was previously unknown, and Jesus did talk of a rapture in Matthew 24, Paul is showing a very different rapture where Christians will not go through the tribulation. Remember the rapture of Matthew 24 is different in that Jews have to go through the tribulation and be raptured afterwards.

PAUL'S MINISTRATION TO
THE JEWS

Although Paul's ministry was primarily for the Gentile, he did deal with some Jews. This explains why Hebrews—if Paul wrote it—contained some end-time Jewish teachings. He writes in Hebrews 1:2, "Hath in the last days..." referring to the end-times. The title of the book also suggests its contents are for Jews. If it is about Jewish end-time doctrines, it will naturally be a faith-and-works system again.

In Hebrews 10:26–27, it is written, "For if we sin wilfully after that we have received the knowledge of the truth, there remaineth no more sacrifice for sins, But a certain fearful looking for of judgment and fiery indignation, which shall devour the adversaries." This verse suggests you will go to hell if you sin. It also contradicts Paul's teaching of salvation by faith alone. This is because the two verses refer to end-time Jews, not the Church.

Nevertheless, Hebrews contains Christian doctrines as well.

PART 3
- CHRISTIANS

Romans to Philemon and matching verses

<hr />

W e, the Church, primarily get our doctrines from Paul, who wrote primarily for the Gentiles. If Paul wrote Hebrews, he did teach some end-time Jewish doctrine as well. This is also seen in Acts.

The Holy Ghost baptism was received by physical deeds, not by faith in Jesus Christ, as they were dealing physically with physical Jews. When Paul found certain disciples, they told him "We have not so much as heard whether there be any Holy Ghost" (Acts 19:1–2). Thus, they did not receive the Holy Ghost beforehand. Why was this so? For they were baptized "Unto John's baptism" (Acts 19:3). John the Baptist's ministry was primarily Jewish. He practiced physical water baptism for physical Jews for the sake of letting Jews receive the things of God.

Notice that when "they were baptized in the name of the Lord Jesus...the Holy Ghost came on them; and they spake with tongues, and prophesied" (Acts 19:4–6). Charismatics and Pentecostals use this verse to claim you have to be baptized by water to receive the Holy Ghost and that you will receive signs afterward. However, these verses were addressed to Jews, specifically those from John's baptism. Physical signs are for physical Jews.

Since Paul ministered to some Jews, he was also able to perform signs and wonders. Spiritual Christians lack signs, but signs still existed as physical Jews were still present. Paul said in Romans 15:18–19,

> *"For I will not dare to speak of any of those things which Christ hath not wrought by me, to make the Gentiles obedient, by word and deed, Through mighty signs and wonders, by the power of the Spirit of God; so that from Jerusalem, and round about unto Illyricum, I have fully preached the gospel of Christ."*

Notice Paul was able to do physical signs by the spirit of God. It also reveals he still ministered to the Jews at the same time as to the Gentiles, which along with the fact that Paul is a Jew himself explains why he can do signs and wonders.

The physical nation of Israel and the physical Jews are done with, as seen when Paul writes in Romans 11:25, "For I would not, brethren, that ye should be ignorant of this mystery, lest ye should be wise in your own conceits; that blindness in part is happened to Israel, until the fulness of the Gentiles be come in."

However, it is temporary, as God will come and save Israel in the future: "And so all Israel shall be saved: as it is written, There shall come out of Sion the Deliverer, and shall turn away ungodliness from Jacob" (Romans 11:26). God gave a promise to Abraham a long time ago, saying that His covenant with physical Israel will never be broken. Hence, God will use physical Israel again.

SPIRITUAL DEALINGS OF THE CHRISTIAN CHURCH

ᔐᕦᔐᕬ

Since we Christians are dealt with spiritually, our dealings will be about the spirit. Hence, we retrieve doctrines from spiritual teachings. Since Paul ministered primarily to Gentiles, we must look at his writings, specifically the books from Romans to Philemon. These books make an introduction to the Gentiles and make mention of the Christian Church.

However, God dealt spiritually even before Paul. For example, Abraham's faith when he believed God is spiritual. Another is that the works of the law were imperfect. Yet another is that from Matthew to John, Jesus was introducing spiritual doctrines and salvation by faith alone and the spiritual kingdom of God.

The apostles taught some spiritual things that are applicable to the Christians as well. Hence, whatever verse in the Bible that matches Romans to Philemon will be a spiritual Christian doctrine. This is why Paul had to find every spiritual dealing in the Old Testament to prove his own spiritual Christian doctrine and put it in Romans to Philemon.

The law, water baptism, and receiving of the baptism of the Holy Ghost through physical deeds are gone for the Christian church, because they are for the physical Jew. This is why Paul said we do not go by the law for our salvation: "Blotting out the handwriting of ordinances that was against us, which was contrary to us, and took it out of the way, nailing it to his cross" (Colossians 2:14). Jewish physical diets, rules of the Mosaic Law, and days of observances are not applicable anymore.

Water baptism is no longer required for salvation, "For Christ sent (Paul) not to baptize but to preach the gospel..." (1 Corinthians 1:17). Paul is saying that the gospel of salvation does not involve water baptism because Christians' salvation is spiritual and faith-based.

We also receive the Holy Spirit by faith in the Lord Jesus Christ, not by the laying on of hands or baptism: "For by one spirit are we all baptized into one body" (1 Corinthians 12:13). How do you receive the Spirit into body of Christ? By faith in the gospel of the Lord Jesus Christ. "That the Gentiles should be fellowheirs, and of the same body, and partakers of his promise in Christ by the gospel" (Ephesians 3:6). This verse clearly says you enter the body by the gospel. Entrance by baptism is left unmentioned.

We do also practice water baptism, but it is based on spiritual dealings. The spiritual aspect of water baptism is in doing it in good conscience. In 1 Peter 3:21, Peter writes, "The like figure whereunto even baptism doth also now save us (not the putting away of the filth of the flesh, but the answer of a good conscience toward God)...." Hence, we practice water baptism not for salvation by works like the Jews but for the spiritual respect of possessing a good conscience. Note how even water baptism contains a spiritual aspect—hyper-dispensationalists wrongly reject water baptism.

Christians follow the law only when it relates to our spiritual walk with Jesus Christ. Hence, we do not observe rituals like the Sabbath or diets, only laws concerning spiritual matters.

50

"For all the law is fulfilled in one word, even in this; Thou shalt love thy neighbour as thyself...Walk in the Spirit, and ye shall not fulfill the lust of the flesh" (Galatians 5:14–16). See how the keeping of the law is dependent on your spiritual walk with Jesus. Furthermore, the laws we follow are those relating to our spiritual walk with Christ, such as "thou shalt not kill," not those that mention observances. By following the Holy Spirit and not the flesh, you are automatically keeping the law. Hyper-dispensationalists err again in ignoring the law, which is important for helping Christians' spiritual walk, seen in laws such as those against murder and homosexuality.

For Christians today, what should be the final authority for our beliefs? It is the Bible, not physical signs. All our doctrine stems from the Bible, the spiritual Word of God.

"Blessed be the God and father of our Lord Jesus Christ who hath blessed us with all spiritual blessings in heavenly places in Christ" (Ephesians 1:3). We can receive spiritual blessings from Old Testament books and General Epistles. Thus, we should not ignore them but instead retrieve spiritual blessings contained within them and apply to ourselves while disregarding the portions written for end-time Jews.

MODERN TEACHINGS TO AVOID

---・ྀ・ི・---

We must avoid the Mid-Acts/Hyper-dispensationalists/Grace Church. They ignore the spiritual Christian doctrines found in the Old Testament, which can give us spiritual blessings.

Avoid those heretics who teach water baptism for salvation— Roman Catholics, the Church of Christ, the Mormons, and some Pentecostals.

Some say the plan of salvation has been the same from beginning to end. That is Covenant Theology/Covenant of Grace. This is held primarily by Calvinists, Presbyterian Churches, James White, and even some Independent Fundamental Baptist churches, such as Shelton Smith, Sword of the Lord, Jack Hyles and his churches, and West Coast Baptist College under Paul Chappell, among others. They teach this heresy.

Those who teach Christians are to be raptured after the tribulation are also heretics. That is an end-times Jewish doctrine, as seen previously. Kent Hovind, Texe Marrs, Catholics, and many cults teach this.

Lordship salvation teaches that having faith in Christ is not enough for salvation, but that faith in Christ must be followed up with a significant change of carnal behavior. This is heresy.

There are still carnal saved Christians. John MacArthur, Paul Washer, Ray Comfort, and James White, among others, teach this heresy. Remember that for Christians, our salvation is still faith alone, even when still sinning. These false teachers gained their doctrine from Bible passages that were meant for different time periods or from something Jewish.

Many also teach works for salvation. Teachers of this heresy include every single religion except Baptist denominations: Catholics, Masons, Buddhists, Hindus, Seventh Day Adventists, Jehovah's Witnesses, Mormons, Scientologists, and the Church of Christ.

Some teach you can lose your salvation from committing a sin after salvation. This is heresy because Christians are saved by faith, even when still sinning. Again, they retrieve verses from some other time period or Jewish matters.

Heretics who teach signs: Charismatics, Pentecostals, Catholics, Benny Hinn, Joel Osteen, famous TBN preachers, Bishop T. D. Jakes and John Hagee. Teaching signs is heresy as Christians are under spiritual dealings by faith in the Word of God and not signs and wonders—physical signs are for the physical Jew.

People who teach you have to receive the baptism of the Holy Ghost by physical actions such as the laying on of hands and water baptism are also heretics. These physical deeds were meant for a different time period and different group of people (Jews). Christians are based on spiritual dealings.

Teachers of Replacement Theology, which claims the church replaces Israel, are heretics as well, as the Church only replaces Israel temporarily, while physical Israel will be dealt with again since God promised Abraham he will never forsake physical Israel. Calvinists, Texe Marrs, and many cults believe this.

Seventh-Day Adventists and Messianic Jews believe the Sabbath and law observance are required for salvation. This is heresy because Christians are based on spiritual dealings, and these physical dealings are under a different time period or to a Jew.

Old Testament Judaism, where Jesus Christ is not believed to be a suffering Messiah nor that salvation is by faith alone in Christ, is also heresy, because the Old Testament prophesied the Messiah will come as King and Sufferer. Hence, we believe in the first and second coming of Christ, where Christ first came as Sufferer and will come as King later. They also ignore some spiritual dealings of God in the Old Testament, such as those used by Paul.

Prosperity Gospel teachers claim that when you serve God, you will become physically rich. This is heresy as the doctrine of physical prosperity involves a Jew in a different time period. This is taught by Joel Osteen, Rick Warren, Bill Hybels, various megachurches, Bishop T. D. Jakes, Charismatics, non-denominational churches, and new evangelical churches.

Why did we go through this list? To show you that these teachings were of a different time period where physical Jews were involved. All false doctrines err in this area, and that is why we do not follow them. We base the foundation of our doctrines on Romans to Philemon and matching verses because they are addressed to Gentiles and discuss the spiritual dealings of God, not the physical dealings of Israel.

Do not get your doctrines from Genesis 1–3, Genesis 4–50, Job, Exodus to Malachi, Matthew to John, Acts, James to Revelation and Hebrews unless the verse is a spiritual Christian verse that matches Romans to Philemon. They are all under a different time period and group of people.

If someone pulls out verses from Acts to prove signs, ignore them since the verses contradict Romans to Philemon. If someone uses Matthew 3 and Acts to prove the works of repentance are necessary to receive the Holy Spirit and its gifts, ignore them. If someone uses Matthew 24 for a post-tribulation rapture for Christians, ignore them. If the verses do not match Romans to Philemon, ignore them.

THE SECOND COMING - TRIBULATION

End-Times verses and Revelation

―――――――――― ༄໑໑༅ ――――――――――

Doctrines for this time period are retrieved from end-times verses such as those found in Matthew to John, James to Revelation, and verses in the Old Testament talking about the "latter days."

We know there will be a post-tribulation rapture for Tribulation saints, not Christians, because the church is raptured before the tribulation. Spiritual Christian dealings are gone and replaced by dealings with physical people. The physical nation of Israel will return. Faith and works for salvation as well, as it is a physical dealing.

Revelations 14 shows a rapture after the tribulation. Revelation 7 mentions the twelve tribes of Israel and how Israel will be used again. Revelation 12 and 14 mentions salvation by faith and works. It is written, "here are they that keep the commandments of God, and the faith of Jesus" (Revelation 14:12). During the tribulation, you also have to avoid the mark of the beast, which is a work.

THE MILLENNIUM KINGDOM

Kingdom verses and Revelation

───────── ༄ৎৎ৫ ─────────

God promised a kingdom. Remember all the kingdom passages in Matthew to John, such as the Sermon on the Mount in Matthew 5 to 7. The prophecy of the Messiah as king finally comes to pass.

It will also be works for salvation, not faith, in this time period. In Hebrews 11:1, it is written, "Now faith is the substance of things hoped for, the evidence of things not seen." Faith is believing without seeing, but in the kingdom, everyone will see Jesus. Thus, faith is not necessary. Works are involved because you will be living under a Holy God in a Holy Kingdom, and you will have to do holy things.

If you are born during this period, you will have to do holy things. Thus, you will be under works salvation. This is seen in Isaiah 33:14–15.

> *"The sinners in Zion are afraid; fearfulness hath surprised the hypocrites. Who among us shall dwell with the devouring fire? who among us shall dwell with everlasting burnings? He that walketh righteously, and speaketh uprightly; he that despiseth*

the gain of oppressions, that shaketh his hands from
holding of bribes, that stoppeth his ears from hearing
of blood, and shutteth his eyes from seeing evil...."

The verses say that you escape hellfire by doing good works.
We know this is talking about the context of Jesus during the
kingdom, for Isaiah states not long after, "Thine eyes shall see
the king in his beauty: they shall behold the land that is very
far off" (Isaiah 33:17). The king has come.

CONCLUSION

"Study to shew thyself approved unto God, a workman that needeth not to be ashamed, rightly dividing the word of truth" (2 Timothy 2:15).

Study the Bible like God told you to in the above verse—by the proper division of the Bible. Without division, you will combine everything, and you will not understand a single thing in the Bible. Many do not divide. No wonder many see Christianity as a joke and the Bible as rife with contradictions.

Here is good advice: when a person quotes a verse and teaches a doctrine, if the verse matches word-for-word the doctrine being taught, believe him. If the verse does not match the doctrine word-for-word, do not believe him.

Heretics do not leave the verses as they say but reinterpret them to reconcile contradictions and problems in the Bible. They do so out of necessity as they do not divide the Word. The division of the Word, however, will solve all contradictions and problems without changing Scripture. God's Word should never be corrected. We left every verse alone yet solved every problem because we divided the Word.

If I tell my brother to wash the dishes and my sister not to wash the dishes, is there a contradiction? Or is it contradictory that ancient Greece punished stealing by death while modern Greece punished stealing by imprisonment? Definitely not in

61

either case. It is common sense that if you consider the right person or the right time period, there will be no contradiction.

Satan says in Isaiah 14:14, "I will ascend above the heights of the clouds; I will be like the most High." Will I claim this verse applies to me? No, because Satan spoke that verse, not me. We know we are of the spiritual, non-Jewish Christian church under Romans to Philemon. If we are shown Acts 2:38 (repent and be baptized for the remission of sins), Matthew 24 (a post-tribulation rapture) or James 2 (do faith and works for salvation), we know that they do not apply to us, because they contradict who we are in Romans-Philemon. We are obviously not Jews under different dispensations. It is similar to how Isaiah 14 does not apply to us, because it contradicts who we are. We are obviously not Lucifer in a different dispensation.

Dispensationalism is a common, basic rule.

ABOUT THE AUTHOR

———— ꝺꞒꝺꞒ ————

Dr Gene Kim is a pastor at San Jose Bible Baptist Church. He believes in dispensationalism, KJV onlyism and Bible Believing truth. He has earned his Bachelor, Master's and Doctorate degrees at Pensacola Bible Institute, Florida and the University of Berkeley, California.

He has over ten years of experience working in five ministries and pastoring two churches. After studying and debating with hundreds of atheists, religionists, and the highly educated and deceived Christians, he is firmly convinced that REAL Bible-believing Christianity is the only truth and promising joy in this world. It is his heavy burden to show this to the billions deceived in darkness.

To find out more about Dr Gene Kim, please visit the following pages:

www.realbiblebelievers.com

https://www.youtube.com/c/REALBibleBelievers/

Made in the USA
Monee, IL
25 March 2022